MW01199970

ZHENG XIAOQIONG was born in Nanchong, Sichuan, in 1980, and moved south to Guangdong at the age of twenty-one to work in the factories. Her poetry has been published in *People's Literature*, *Poetry Magazine*, *Independence*, and *Piston*. She has published several collections of poetry; her work has been translated into a dozen languages and received many awards, including the prestigious People's Literature Award. She has been invited to events around the world, from the Singapore International Migrant Arts Festival to the Rotterdam Poetry Festival. Her poetry has been set to music and dramatized, with performances in the United States, Germany, and elsewhere.

ELEANOR GOODMAN is the author of the poetry collection *Nine Dragon Island*, which was a finalist for the 2016 Drunken Boat First Book Prize, and the forthcoming *Lessons in Glass*. She is the translator of five books from Chinese, including *Something Crosses My Mind: Selected Poems of Wang Xiaoni*, which was the recipient of a 2013 PEN/Heim Translation Fund Grant and winner of the 2015 Lucien Stryk Asian Translation Prize. Her anthology *Iron Moon*, a translation of Chinese migrant workers' poetry, was named a book of the year in *The Times Literary Supplement*. She is a research associate at the Fairbank Center for Chinese Studies at Harvard University and was awarded a National Endowment for the Arts Translation Fellowship.

Zheng Xiaoqiong

In the Roar of the Machine
Selected Poems

TRANSLATED FROM THE CHINESE AND WITH
AN INTRODUCTION BY ELEANOR GOODMAN

NYRB/POETS

 NEW YORK REVIEW BOOKS   *New York*

THIS IS A NEW YORK REVIEW BOOK
PUBLISHED BY THE NEW YORK REVIEW OF BOOKS
207 East 32nd Street, New York, NY 10016
www.nyrb.com

First published in Australia by the Giramondo Publishing Company.

Library of Congress Cataloging-in-Publication Data
Names: Zheng, Xiaoqiong, 1980– author. | Goodman, Eleanor, 1979–
    translator.
Title: In the roar of the machine / by Zheng Xiaoqiong; translated from
    the Chinese by Eleanor Goodman.
Description: New York: New York Review Books, 2025. | Series: NYRB
    poets
Identifiers: LCCN 2025007908 (print) | LCCN 2025007909 (ebook) | ISBN
    9781681379388 (paperback) | ISBN 9781681379395 (ebook)
Subjects: LCSH: Zheng, Xiaoqiong, 1980– —Translations into English. |
    Factories—Poetry. | LCGFT: Poetry.
Classification: LCC PL2977.5.E6436 I53 2025 (print) | LCC PL2977.5.E6436
    (ebook) | DDC 895.11/6—dc23/eng/20250305
LC record available at https://lccn.loc.gov/2025007908
LC ebook record available at https://lccn.loc.gov/2025

ISBN 978-1-68137-938-8
Available as an electronic book; ISBN 978-1-68137-939-5

Cover and book design by Emily Singer

The authorized representative in the EU for product safety and compliance
is eucomply OÜ, Pärnu mnt 139b-14, 11317 Tallinn, Estonia,
hello@eucompliancepartner.com, +33 757690241.

Printed in the United States of America on acid-free paper.
10 9 8 7 6 5 4 3 2 1

Contents

INTRODUCTION

ZHENG XIAOQIONG'S POETRY brings to the fore issues of Chinese domestic migration, global capitalism and income disparity, the contemporary Chinese poetry scene, geopolitics and the world economy, feminism, wage discrimination, and workers' rights. Quite aside from the sociological import of her work, it is Zheng's own unique poetics that gives life to these issues, providing a powerful experience through which readers can understand and empathize with often overlooked people, including workers, women, and the rural poor. Although Zheng has published several books and her work has been enthusiastically received in China and in international poetry circles, her poetry has typically been viewed under a narrow rubric, namely that of "migrant worker poetry" and the "migrant worker poet." While this is where Zheng's literary career began, it is only one part of the story of Zheng's life and work.

In the Chinese context, "migrant worker" refers to an enormous "floating workforce" that comprises one of the largest human migrations in recorded history. Zheng Xiaoqiong herself took part in this enormous flow of people from the rural areas to the industrial zones. She was born in a mountainous region of Sichuan in 1980, and after training as a nurse and working briefly in a hospital there, she left home to seek work in the factories of Dongguan, a southern Chinese city known as one of the workshops (or sweatshops) of the world.

Overwhelmed by what she encountered in the hardware factory where she first found employment, Zheng turned to writing as a release from emotional and psychological pressure, but also as a form of protest and witness. From the start, she wrote across genres, producing essays, fiction, informal reportage, and poetry; the juxtaposition and melding of these different modes of writing are characteristic of her style. Her poems sometimes seem to slip towards prose, and her ability to capture voices and experiences that are not her own shows an ear highly attuned to both song and narration. Much of her work comes from her own direct experience or observation, and pulsates with linguistic, moral, and narrative intensity.

What you don't know is that my name has been
    hidden by an employee ID
my hands become part of the assembly line, my body
    signed over
to a contract, my black hair is turning white, leaving
    noise and toil
overtime work and wages . . . I've passed through
    fixed fluorescent lights
and the exhausted shadows flung on the machine
    stations move slowly
turning, bending down, silent as cast iron

The employee ID, sometimes with a name, more often only with a worker's assigned number, conceals rather than testifies to an individual's identity. This destruction of the individual, and the resulting loss of autonomy and agency, inform much of Zheng's work. These "exhausted shadows" work in concert with the machines, and must fight to maintain their humanity within a deeply dehumanizing system.

Zheng has resisted the limitations of the moniker of "migrant worker poet," however, and the concomitant role assigned to her first by birth and circumstance, and then by the literary establishment. Most of her poems having to do with the factory involve a larger context, whether it be globalization, feminism, or environmental degradation. She has also produced a significant body of work that has little to do with factory life and its human cost. The poems here from her collection *Rose Courtyard* depart from the world of the assembly line and work stations. These poems are replete with classical literary allusions and historical references, and often read like extended allegories or even fairytales. The characters are loosely based on Zheng's own relatives, including a paternal grandfather who took five wives. But the history and culture of Sichuan also play a role, demonstrating Zheng's engagement not only with the present but also the past, and the ways in which the past lives on in personal memory and in the culture. This poetry is also threaded with symbols and tropes quite different from those found in Zheng's factory poems. Instead of iron, assembly lines, occupational diseases, and dismemberment, readers encounter flower petals, embroidery, gardens, birds, and withered branches, along with hints of the stifled female aspiration endemic in eras in which women were allowed little role outside of the home. Yet despite the impressive breadth these poems represent in Zheng's oeuvre, some of the underlying concerns remain the same:

> I return to the courtyard, carrying three damp books
> and feminist thoughts unsuited to the time
> longing for the old days of the courtyard, the five
>   grandmothers
> with their love and disparate fortunes

"Feminist thoughts" were unwelcome a century ago in rural China, and they are still discouraged by those in power on the factory floor and in many other contexts. The speaker here is estranged from the courtyard and its residents by her books and her thoughts as much as her age and experiences. Yet the accessibility of archetypal stories—thwarted love, frustrated ambition, the interactions of the natural world with the human realm—underpin these poems and lend them a sense of the universal, despite their particular Sichuanese and Chinese contexts.

In this collection, one of my main goals as Zheng Xiao-qiong's translator has been to bring Zheng's literary activism to a Western audience. To do so requires an awareness of the intersections of cultural, economic, and social factors that are at play in Zheng's work and life. She writes from a strongly feminist, working-class, rural Chinese background, yet her breadth of experience and range of reference are much wider. To translate her poetry requires a knowledge not only of the vocabulary of the factory and the urban village, but an attention to her delicate gradations of tone and diction, which address the lives of migrant workers and also engage with classical Chinese poetry, global inequality, her family history within its complex cultural context, and the flora and fauna of her home. Most important, however, is Zheng's voice, which can be tender, urgent, imploring, regretful, and learned in equal measure. I hope these translations offer all that and much more to the reader.

—*Eleanor Goodman*

Huangmaling (2006)

Life

What you don't know is that my name has been hidden by
    an employee ID
my hands become part of the assembly line, my body
    signed over
to a contract, my black hair is turning white, leaving noise
    and toil
overtime work and wages ... I've passed through fixed
    fluorescent lights
and the exhausted shadows flung on the machine stations
    move slowly
turning, bending down, silent as cast iron
iron that speaks in sign language, covered with the
    disappointment and grief of migrants
iron that rusts over time, iron that trembles in the midst
    of reality—
I don't know how to protect a silent life
this life of a lost name and gender, this life of surviving off
    of contracts
where and how do I start, with the moon on the metal
    cots in the eight-person dorm room
what it illuminates is homesickness, the secret flirting
    and love in the roar of the machines,
or youth stopped by a timesheet, and how in the middle of
    this restless life
can one console a frail soul, if the moonlight comes from
    Sichuan
then my childhood is lit by memories, extinguished by a
    seven-day assembly line work week
what's left, these blueprints, iron, metal products, or white

inspection labels, red defective goods, and under the
    fluorescent lights, the loneliness and pain
I bear, in all this toil, hot and endless . . .

Huangmaling

I settle my body and soul in this town
its lychee trees, street, one tiny station on its assembly lines
its ideas drenched in rain, trip after trip, time after time,
I find places for my thoughts, my love, my dreams, my
    youth on its surfaces
and my lovers, voices, smells, life
are here away from home, beneath its dim streetlamp
I dash around, I'm soaked in rain and sweat, panting—
I arrange my life on plastic products, screws, nails
on a tiny employee ID...my entire life
I give myself to it, this tiny village
the wind blows away everything I have
all that's left is old age, and returning home

They

I remember this iron, iron that rusted over time
pale red or dark brown, tears in a furnace fire
I remember the distracted, exhausted eyes above the
    workstations
their gazes were small and trivial, small as a gradual
    furnace fire
their depression and distress, and a tiny bit of hope
lit up by the flames, unfolding on white blueprints
or between the red lines of a traditional painting, by the
    meagre monthly wages
and a heart more exhausted by the day—

I remember their faces, their turbulent eyes and subtle
    trembling
their calloused fingers, their rough and simple lives
I say quietly: they are me, I am they
our grief and pain and hope are kept silent and forbearing
our confessions and hearts and loves are in tears,
as silent and lonely as iron, or as pain

I say, in the vast crowds, we are all alike
we all love and hate, we all breathe, we all have noble spirits
we all have unyielding loneliness and compassion!

Machine

That hungry machine, every day eating iron, blueprints
stars, dew, salty sweat, it picks its teeth
and spits out profit, bank notes, nightclubs...it sees
    lopped-off fingers
unpaid wages, shadowy occupational diseases, and the
    memories are bitter
and the nights are endless, how many people living on an
    iron sheet
owe the debts of the poor, stand on the cool damp iron
moving about miserably, how much love balances between
    iron sheets
this life's heart is iron-hard, a straightforward bitter life of
    a temporary laborer
she doesn't know how long this starlight and darkness,
    these objects with their shadows
will stay before dropping away, before revealing their
    sensitive delicate hearts
with enormous machines on their backs   the gloomy
    hidden roar
like love, like hate, like pain, like the moonlight hidden
    between iron and steel
the threads that send forth life   hiss   grow old
their aging veins soak in the years' rust
fate is like those small gentle hands   on a hard workstation
a quiet life   its blue flames illuminating your exhausted
    face

Iron Tools

Grey
enormous iron anchors toss in her green dreams
deafening roars, rocking
bent iron sheets with the sunlight falling on the machines
her scapulae protrude into empty afternoons
the green dreams of pregnancy she once had
are gone amid spiralling grey bits of iron
millions of bits of iron warped under steel ingots
she sees she's just a piece of extruded iron
bent and shaped on a temporary workstation
on the spinning of the nuts
within the interweaving of sound and light
she is turned, ground, lifted, milled by life...
she can't refuse these enormous forces that heat and forge
at last, she sees herself branded by the burning hot steel
    plate: *Passed inspection!*

Drama

She extracts a wide wilderness from her body
burying disease and moodiness, planting glimmering words
steadfast, calm, believing, installing inside her body
a high-powered machine, it bores into time
eating through her youth and enthusiasm, and it produces
her fake fat life, this sorrow
or depression from being trapped, and it soaks her
in fabricated pain, while others imagine her life
her shabby clothes, to be like a classical
tragedy, but really her days are ordinary though difficult
each tiny interior holds a silent soul
she writes poetry at the machine of the Chinese language,
    this ancient
but fictitious vehicle. She places herself
at a workstation on the assembly line, an employee number
replacing her name and gender, and with that machine she
    grinds and cuts
her heart full of love and complaint, some even think
you can find the depth of the times in these little moods
but she hides inside her thin small body, using everything up
to love herself, these landscapes, these rivers and epochs
these battles, capital, scenery, to her
they mean less than a love affair, she will get used to
twelve-hour workdays, clocking in, the exhaustion
cutting out a single thin life on the revolving machine
using Chinese to record her bloated heart and rage
more often, she stands at the window of some electronics
    factory
her back to her vast country, the dim dirty streetlamps
collecting her heart's loneliness with a machine

Industrial Zone

The fluorescent lights are lit, the buildings are lit, the
    machines are lit exhaustion is lit, the blueprints are lit...
this is a night on an endless work week, this is the night of
    the mid-autumn festival
the moon lights up a disk of emptiness, in the lychee trees
a light breeze sways an interior whiteness, many years of
    speechless
quiet, insects humming in evergreen grasses, the city's lights
    illuminate
the industrial zone, so many dialects, so much homesickness,
so many weak and insubstantial bodies placed there, so
    much moonlight shining
on the endless work week of machines and blueprints, and it
    rises
to shine on my face, a sluggishly dropping heart

So many lamps are lit, so many people pass by
the industrial zone's lamps, past, workstations
the mute moonlight, lamplight, and me
so much paltriness, small as spare parts or filaments
warming the industrial zone's bustle and clamour with their
    feeble bodies

And the tears, the joy, the pain we've had
our glorious or petty thoughts, and our souls
are all illuminated by the moonlight, collected, and carried
    afar
hidden in rays of light no one will notice

Sounds

These sounds I hear, stiff, vertical,
like an enormous iron hammer on an anvil, *clank, clank*
these low sobs, sorrowful, bloated, oppressive
we walk, we run
slowly, our captive fate!
The sounds I hear when I turn are like pieces of cut iron
circular, square, in strips...iron I cannot speak of
it is silent as we sob, life's iron hammer pounds
in the flames of the furnace or the light of daytime
I see myself resembling this cast iron
bit by bit, burnished, cut out, slowly
becoming an unspeaking component, a tool, an apparatus
turning into this voiceless, this silent, this mute life!

Train

My body contains a vast open plain, a train
is travelling across it, but autumn is in its deep
suffering twilight, and I follow the train's
meandering path, planting a thousand hawthorn trees in the
  wilderness
their white crowns and fiery fruit, permeated with humanity
and tranquillity, I know fate is like endless mountains,
  rivers, fields
or a winding river, it wriggles along behind the train
the mountains are covered in a ragged clothing of trees, their
  sparse unconvincing shadows
move with the train, one tree, two trees ... it stops on the
  grey indistinct plain
I say to the trees, that is my friend, my dear one

Workshop

Sawing, cutting
polishing, drilling
milling, lathing
weighing, rolling
cooling off, in a heating bath
biting, severing
carving characters, labelling
the lathe, the milling machine
the planer, the forklift
the cutting machine, the scales
the motors, the coolant
the clamps, the plastic sheeting
the labels, the bandages
the wiring, the incandescent lights
the Yunnan bruise powder, the employee IDs
the permission slips for five minutes in the bathroom
two minutes at the water dispenser
the smell of glue hitting the face, the smell of benzene
the smell of rust, oily smells, the smell of sweat, body odor
the smell of armpits, the scorched smell of burnt packaging
the sleep they can't throw off
distorted, stripped, folded
in pieces, square, thin
thick, circular, in chunks:
the finished products, the half-finished products
repaired products, rejects, spare parts
reset, warehoused, arranged, packaged up
they hear the roaring—
ripping—chugging—
squeaking—squawking—

thumping
thump thump—
thump thump thump—

Time

In the village where I've lived for six years, in the lychee
    grove
the mountain stream shines on my truncated youth
the hardware factory's drowsy dream
leaves Silver Lake Park, heading north
I polish a migrant's sighs
and my own closer Huangmaling dialect
in the shade of banyan trees, the blazing industrial zone
turns brighter and brighter in the minds of the workers
past events fall from memory, wet
with grief, and the lights show the wrinkles slowly
    forming at my eyes
a lonely bird hides itself in the darkness of the lychee grove
the darkness overwhelms the red of the lychees, and the
    dark branches
turn even darker, the birdcalls have faded, and here
the roar of the hardware factory continues its banging
    unabated
my worker's number is 231, when I take the blueprints,
    there in the darkness
in the midst of forgotten time, I see my youth
wriggling away through clean, transparent grief
withering in the vastness of my country

A Product's Story

First, it starts with a warped piece of iron sheeting, setting
    off from a village, iron mine, truck,
steamer, or port, then losing one's name, getting a number,
    standing at a workstation;
second is springs and assembly lines, the whinny of
    nervous motion, pain close by, aluminum alloys,
blueprints, breadcrumbs, cutting machines, familiar sweat,
    plastic and cardboard boxes
and their pleasures and sorrows; third is the pale faces
    under fluorescent lights, employee IDs, mechanical
    springs,
gears, card edge connectors, pressure coolants, anti-rust
    oil, silent overtime;
fourth is certificates, standardized forms, exterior polish-
    ing, the lashings of a 3000-degree furnace
the hot and cold treatment of overtime pay, the rain of
    being fired, your twisted-up
body appearing in an hourglass; fifth is temporary residence
    permits, physical exam cards, proof of single status,
migrant worker cards, work permits ... they wait in line,
    silently, leaning on
plastic travel bags with exhausted faces; sixth is youthful
    pinned-down arms, unpaid wages
and fines, missed periods, a medical history of flus,
    listlessness, homesickness
as wide as the sea, noise from overhead lights, drifting in a
    distant city and payslips floating on a river;
seventh is the dialects of machines and dorms, Hunanese
    dreams on the berth above Sichuanese,
Hubeinese is neighbours with Anhuinese, the Gansunese
    machine bit off half

of the Jiangxinese's finger, Guangxinese's nightshift,
   Guizhounese's gloominess, Yunnanese's rainsoaked
sleep-talk and Henanese's dress. Eighth is fried dough
   sticks, lumps
of instant noodles, the shape of the city in vegetable soup,
   masks made of copper, coupling links, certificates of
   conformity,
a kuai and half of fried rice noodles, chili sauce, artificially
   flavored and colored cola;
ninth is love hidden in stories and fairytales, shared rented
   rooms, doors
without keys, iron ladders to upper berths, antiseptic
   fluids in hospitals, birth control pills, the tears of
   breaking up,
corroded flesh, baseless promises of love; tenth is train
   tickets to go home, a gate
or threshold, a discount ticket or a possible fake, squeezed
   in the aisles,
in the toilet, standing on tiptoe, crushed, you just want to
   find a place on the train or in the world
to live, to love, to slowly grow old

The Assembly Line

Along with the flow of the assembly line is the flow of people
they come from Hedong or Hexi, she stands and sits, with a
    number, blue uniform,
white worker's hat, her fingers on her workstation, her name
    is A234, A967, Q36...
or it's plugger-in, sling-loader, screw-turner...

Crossing between the flow of migrant workers and the flow
    of products,
the women are fish, working night and day, dragging along
the boss's order forms, profit, the GDP, youth, vision, dreams
dragging along the glory of the Industrial Age

In the noise of turnover, they live lonelier lives,
women and men flow past each other as strangers
the women's lives get pushed back in the water, leaving
    screws in their hands, pieces of plastic
iron nails, glue, coughing lungs, bodies wracked with
    occupational diseases, floating in the flow of temporary
    work

The assembly line constantly tightens the valves of the city
    and destiny, those yellow
switches, red wires, grey products, the fifth cardboard box
holds plastic lamps, fake Christmas trees, youthfulness on
    employee IDs, Li Bai's
burning love turned cold, or still reading his poetry softly:
    oh, so romantic!
In its understated flow, I see fate flowing
here in a southern city, I lower my head to write quatrains
    and ballads of this Industrial Age

Witnessed

Noises
of gears
iron sheets
synthesizers
plastics
they roll, scrape, scream, shout

drowsiness grows on her skin at four a.m.

noises
of cutting
polishing
drilling
striking
they flow, walk, run, pause

drowsiness grows in her body at four a.m.

noises
of curses
hearts
yawns
exhaustion
they mix, tangle, twist, pile up

drowsiness grows in her bones at four a.m.

at four a.m. I witnessed her drowsiness grow wooden
I witnessed her finger let the machine take a bite
I witnessed the spray of blood wake her from drowsiness
I witnessed her crying, her screams
I witnessed our sighs, our helplessness

and then, the noises started up again
and then, the drowsiness started to grow again

and then...
came silence

Workshop Love

My fantasies toil away in the dark workshop...
the cast iron machine console thoughtfully droops its
    horsehead top
behind the burnished steel strip   behind the temporary
    darkness and silence
your oily fingers and piercing eyes   your chest
is steady as a hydraulic press—full of scorching pulsing
    passion
tenderness flows from my thick bent fingers...
amber lips   iron   blueprints   bright metal indicators
my tongue   love   torso   switches   the force of a turning
    screwdriver
fate and memory   you in the darkness   sourness of sweat
oil streaks on arms   those strands of messy black hair
blue breakfast smoke caught in the stomach   the cramped
    workshop
I feel the tenderness between calluses   with its rose-red
love...in the messy handwriting on a workshop certificate
what's written in blue ballpoint pen is longing   what's
    written in red
is love   and the white paper shows your oily fingerprints
and your body's warmth   black film   curved slings
the horsehead machine like your shadow   moves slowly
life's machine creaks   love flowing from machines
products on the shelves   violently birthed exhaustion and
    calluses
thick fingers float over a rough life   but love
the only sign of spring in the dark workshop   grows...

Iron

Small iron, soft iron, blown by the wind
pounded by the rain, iron reveals its rusty cowardice and
    timidity
the conclusion of last year...was like time dripping through
    a pinhole
how much iron is still in the night, in the open warehouse,
    on the workstations...where
does it want to go, and where will it be taken? How much
    iron
questions itself at night, how much is
rusting with a rustle, while at night who
claims life's past and future in the midst of their ironlike
    lives

What else doesn't rust? Last year followed a freight car
to someplace far away, this year is still flowing between the
    fingers
next year is a piece of iron about to arrive, awaiting the
    blueprints
machine stations, order forms, but at this moment, where
    am I and where will I go
"Life is like a stove fire burning, roiling."
My outsider's timidity is rusting in my body
in me, a person, a group of people

and a handful of iron, iron that has kept silent for years
iron that can leave at any time, iron that can return at any
    time,
rusting in the rustling flow of time, staring into the distance
yearning to take root like the iron window beside me

*Poems Scattered
on Machines* (2009)

Industrial Age

At the US-owned factory Japanese machines run Brazilian
   mines
to produce iron pieces, Germany's lathes shape France's
coastline, South Korea's shelves are filled with Italian parts
Belgium waits in a corner to make a sale, Spain and
   Singapore
perform inspections, Russia is loaded into a warehouse by
   porters, Africa
stands like raw materials in an open field, and Chile's
   order forms, like its territory,
are long and narrow, my Sichuan dialect is a bit
   old-fashioned, the Xiangxi dialect
is even harder to understand, Fujian's Hokkien can chat
   with Taiwanese
Hong Kong's Cantonese is a mere stop along the way, if I
   want
I can move India, Afghanistan, and Pakistan
closer to Australia, Iraq right up against America
and transport Israel to the middle of the Caribbean nations
England shakes hands with Argentina, Japan, Mexico...
in this Industrial Age, I bustle about each day
peacefully organising the entire world in a factory

In the Electronics Factory

1

In Qiaoli (the intersection of the expressway and a local
     highway,
a landscape of potted evergreens, a marsh where rainwater
     collects)
the dark landscaping laborers live an existence of dust
high-speed buses and trucks carry the time's quick
revolutions, dark asphalt roads, white crosswalks
assembly line workers creeping low as holly, dejectedly
passing by, their lives' dust and misfortune scoured by storms
they discuss years of stagnant wages, the men discuss
finding a better job, weekends off, overtime, the women
     discuss
desire, happiness, sorrow, but they're not
like me, steeped in a nameless self-hatred
discussing the meaninglessness of life, this trivial and
     useless depression

2

Pruned plants stand neatly between electronics factories
white uniforms encase the women's youth, names, beauty
their movements, expressions, gazes, all pruned by the
     assembly line
this is the image they leave me with, under the incandescent
     lights's
shadows enduring the crashing of youth, screws, plastic film
metal sheets dub the action for them, adding realistic
     phrases

to annotate the neat movements, the body cannot forgive
    passion
hidden amid the mess of spare parts, this tiny component
is given immense meaning, the economy, capital
trademarks, order forms, crises, and of course squabbling
love. Clearly, in the electronics factory, this epoch turns
    small
endlessly small . . . so small it is just a standard dual tube

3

Drilling machines drill the future out of iron, dreams are
    projected
through the tiny holes, red transistors, green circuits,
golden magnetic recording heads, their smallness, their
    tininess
we live between each little trifle or mediocrity
yes, living, nobodies, weaklings, but we
live, the nearby crowds that come and go
they live in my poetry, on paper, immense
yet frail, the tiny voices of these sentences
these fragile hearts, unable to touch immense things
for these people living without voices
we maintain an ancient pity, but we cannot change
the silent unconcern this era has for them

The Mutating Villages

The wind and its heading, the hand and its palm, or you, him
who is who, and who am I? Hey, who is he?
Where did you come from? Where are you going? Hey, why'd
you come here? Why are you going there?
You've been forgotten by twisted time, you've been
forgiven by the twisted world. Their turbulent
restlessness, where will desire take you, occasionally
the sunset brings truckloads of great and glorious moments
a horse weeps on the riverbank, and in its
grey eyes I find solace, beneath its hooves
the world and maple leaves fall, beneath its hooves,
the world is like a microcosm of a human life, and in the
    end the wind
stirs the grey distant hills, the grey dusky town
the horse away from home bows his head and stands in the
    enormous setting sun
the clop of his hooves meanders like the mountain range
my eyes tangle with time, the minutes pile up in a mountain
and rush in from some distant place, like a galloping horse
that shares my soul and stands between us
as the wind carries the waning September. A whiff of
    farming from the earth
like a white horse's rich breath. This is the twenty-first
    century
this is grey machines and felled lychee groves
they are toppled, courtyards are turned to rubble, earth's
    ruins
the vast earth is roasted in industry's flames, piling up
clusters of buildings, factories, concrete, from the soil to me,
from mechanical arms to my arms, corn leaves, rice paddies,
my flesh, bones, skin, hair all become part of the machine

"an emaciated rice paddy" seems foolish, it reaches out
pure white roots, wanting to seize the feet of the
    Industrial Age
along with a diamond-like soul, my soul
it still stands praying within the fixed fate of life and death
the winds of industry stir, I can't bear it
all the hearts yearning for the past, waiting or cursing
if you're standing, you're part of it
the wind brings the smell of gasoline and the roar of the
    machines
some sort of scene or some sort of story
will the present that we curse become the past that we
    long for
how are morning agriculture and afternoon industry
    different
the earth has tasted human misery, and all that's left is
    "September's long sob
its tears gone," it drowns itself in its own tears
I can't know your pain now, or your tears
in the recesses of steel-reinforced cement, find peace
in the mirror of the water, your dark shadow
runs past like a shining horse, leaving a shadow behind on
    the machines
five years of iron and the sounds of iron, an ant's fate
they migrate restlessly, from the inland to the coast
from villages to cities (Nanchong, Dongguan, or the
    hardware factories of steel cities
to work as operators, lose fingers, a thirty-year-old cook
    and a guard carrying on
an affair in a kitchen corner) a truck setting off loaded
    with endless
assembly lines, thinking of Africa, a distant trap
it's only an iron tool from Africa
where will the wind take you, instants destroyed by time

I see dimly the truck that took away my lost youth
people and villages disturbed by urbanization
they cannot stand without support, the toppled crops and
    trees,
irrigation ditches choked with gravel, shapeshifting time
closes its wings, thunder rolls down from the sheet iron
    roofs
tranquility unfolds its mysterious handprint towards the
    constellations
the stars fall towards the streetlamps's dusty yellow abyss
youth swoops from the branches
tangled time twines with the morning glory
a white flower bud interlocks with rouged surmises
its distorted branches and leaves stop on a faraway
    mountain pass
winds from afar blow on the Tropic of Cancer
it is spring, it stops inside childhood
the same wind is in the rouged elms and peach blossoms
a heart steeped in boundless brilliance
the sunlight gathers dust in its obsolescence
people stand in the dust waiting for something
they hide themselves on the tree-lined boulevards of
    history
and are forgotten, and if one day a pair of focusing pupils
alights on them, or they're replaced in slow motion
some dim plot will carve out memories like a seared brand
so many people bused out to other places
so many people bused in to this village
we're searching for a place further and bigger than home
its former owners have gone away, leaving just like us
is there a town or village where we've lived
that will wait for us, and will welcome them
yet another bus brings us back, aging now, and melancholy
    overcomes me

how long will it take to put down roots here
for this to become my home, when my eyes are filled
with dark ruins, demolished buildings, and all I've wasted—
youth, adversity, the beautiful past
wasted, smashed, gradually dissipating inside my body
my aging thoughts, determination, exhausted body
my loose bones have soaked for ages in the ruins of the
    world
no choice but to surrender, as my blood flows slower
I grow old amid the same repeated actions
the same speed, the same decay advancing daily
teeth loosen, the eyes blur, the old boulders of ideals
are jostled by time, by the days and years remaining
misfortune and fear accumulate between my body and soul
now, I no longer hope for a further, bigger place
that will take me in, time will cruely harvest me
I'll spend the rest of my life in this city, finding a niche
    between buildings
to plant my green life in the desolate earth
and in that narrow niche I'll maintain from the corrupted
    world
half a finger's length of distance, as time carves out a
    moment's nothingness
and spring flashes out on the tip of a branch

Those swinging doors, the wounds of memories
the past illuminates bones
this soon to be reconstructed village
the stench that drifts along the canals
window looking out onto window
people standing in windows watching the street
on the street, I look up at the windows
and the mosaic walls that won't leave any trace of these
    years

a fading history stands underneath a banyan tree
ancient nursery rhymes and allusions have disappeared
the sky no longer flits through a pair of shining eyes
leaves sway in the air, sitting at the door of a hair salon
prostitutes play cards, and their heavily powdered faces
their lipstick and perfume flood into a six-year-old's
     memory
children of poor working women and their commerce-
     distorted childhoods
are like untimely lines of poetry that probe at a sleepy
     reality
if history could be told in just one day, these heroes and
     ordinary people
would turn into corpses in stasis, and would no longer be
     sad
nor dazzling, a car passes by, the rain
wets rusting bones, once belonging to the village landowners
someone singing in the rain gets knocked down, the flowers
     asleep on the sill
return to their twisting green dreams in the silence
the sun and I live back to back, the raw wind
stirs the windowpane, the lychee trees in the courtyard
     stretch
into the books in my gloomy room
they shake hands with an allusion and a plot in a book
both fabricating their background and movements
billowing waves jostle the bed, or the bookshelves
dawn glistens with green shimmers of water
the organisms that swim in my body spy on me
with pairs of eyes born from my body
their pupils like glistening leaves in the green light
in their dark corner, they make sketches
and drawings for my gloomy spirit, their gazes crisscross
duplicate, reflect, oh, this torturous memory

a tattoo on the face of exiles, an eclipse of shock
leaves behind confusion lovely as sealing wax, a deformed
    room
whose windows open to the sky's stars, the heart's laws
fields, villages, cities, every pedestrian, a banquet of books
morality, desire, the gleam of twisted thoughts
a soul like an illuminated seashell, in between poetry and
    me
time builds a high wall, I keep coughing, disease returns to
    the body from afar
if it's not that you're too close, it's not that you're too far
this empty time, these walls in the veins
you can hear the clamor of green leaves on the balcony
the sheen they reflect, a pale green sheen
extends ten emerald fingers, and grasps bizarre imagination
someone sent in from afar a dawn bruised by night
a dignified and holy wound spits out the sun
a drowsy old man stands on top of terrible documents
he's vacant, his brain empty
sitting at his desk, his fantasies are endless
civil servants are used to distracted days
their faces are cold as official documents, bloated by the
    times
relying on rubber stamps and confidential documents,
    bureaucrats
and their fat bodies, green mosaics and glass
nine-storey village committee buildings are interspersed
    with dismal shacks
I uselessly seek the voices of the old fields and gardens
the rainy day swallows, the ancestors of Tomb Sweeping
    Day
Scorpio in the sky, teary-eyed comets dragging their tails
sweeping across the lychee groves, Leo's meteor showers
    wet the banana leaves

insects humming the rhythm of The Beatles, white jade
oracle-bone inscriptions through leaves, the heavens and
plains
are covered with the rust spots of constellations,
surrounded by tranquility
the dusk piles up on a sliced-off mountaintop in the cooling
gloom
the day decomposes in the mountain's shadow, the kind
faces of the oaks
youthful memories fade, the dismembered mountain
behind them
quivers in the roar of the pile driver, its old smile
is not so far away, standing in distant view...confronting me
eternal peace is toppled in an instant, enameled faces
grope at the countryside
partridges bring in the past, stars and mountain ghosts
disappear in the neon lights
house after house turns to fine powder, person after person
enters the yellow earth
souls missing for years gather by brooks and banyan trees
only to collapse in an instant, thousands of years of pre-
served traditions
fall and keep falling, excavators extend their enormous iron
sawteeth
severing the distant umbilical cord between my ancestors
and me
the ancestors enter the deepest dark,
what else can we expect
what else can we value
silken honors rise on the wind like pigeons
empty fields, crop fields about to be dismembered
last year's discarded seed corn is left in the cobwebbed
weeds

it sways in the wind, staring
at the dimmed lychees, the felled trees, the branches
lie around the machine's arm, and the nearly subjugated
    earth
has been severed by excavators all along the village's
    remote paths
the asphalt roads gleam slickly in the afternoon sun, the
    empty fields
the unleveled hillocks and lychee trees stubbornly stand
    tall

On this crowded and utterly conquered earth
chaotic dark clusters of buildings spread
these people hurrying about in the darkness
their dazed and exhausted faces, face after numb face
bankers, directors, dancing girls, officials, managers
artists, singers, businessmen, seekers
bakers, fast food workers, hairdressers, bank tellers,
in the city's darkness is a face made by industry
a blurry and monstrous face, a face stuffed with commerce
    and industry
the trees by the road cling fast to gaps in the cement
fishbone antennas receive riddles from the sky
a melancholy clamor and dubious light from hair salons
secrets buried in dark penthouse corners
the aluminum doors of banks and the golden pillars of
    restaurants
sobbing in the murky corner of a building at dusk
the moon, absent stars, *China Securities Daily*
sauna girls at the Prince Hotel, board chairmen of compa-
    nies going public
the howl of the stock market and real estate, the low cry
    of dark hovels
the funeral of a VIP, the respectful rain

the attendees, the hearse, the casket, a drop of rain
carries his spirit up to heaven, a drop of rain carries his body
down into the earth, in the darkness, you fumble at the
     prison chains
the policeman's electric baton, the sun forms an embryo
     in the dark
ruins from demolition, a stage set for the human world
the play has begun, put out the lights
we come and go like actors
serious, laughing, exaggerated faces
and behind each exhausted face is a heart fabricated by
     this moment
steeped in nothingness, in the shadow of industrial
     buildings and commercial capital
person after person is enslaved, rushing around panic
     stricken
in the grotesque excitement, pedestrians become slaves,
slaves to houses, slaves to vehicles ... sticking out
     mechanical arms that grab my hand
any clear consciousness is tormented by the narcotic of
     profit
she slowly loses her sensitivity
her soul says: hey, quiet down
her heart still surges
she's from the countryside and has a delicate hyper-
     sensitivity
she feels love and hate, with oppression all around her
this era is a high-speed turbine, in turmoil
these throngs not knowing where they're going, in turmoil
this hapless love, belief, hope ... all in turmoil
the insects press their faces to the dark balconies
all the faces become one face
each individual face becomes the face of the crowd

falling into darkness from the light, returning into the
    light from the darkness
among dancing bodies and stilled souls
you separate yourself from yourself
all the clear-cut local species are weeping
planting evergreens and lawns, winter snows
goodbye, grains and fruit trees, brooks, locusts and banyan
    trees
goodbye chirping cicadas, green grasses, the purple-cloud
    fragrance of youth
laughter not yet lost, drainage stations, rural highways
the beer ads on oak bars as dusk barrels in like a train
its white foam spreads like black asphalt roads
those fields not yet gone, those people, middle-aged
newly landless farmers gather under the trees to remem-
    ber, the memories not yet faded
the stubbornness that takes root in reinforced concrete,
    changes to the paper and TV
modernization, the orchestra of economic indicators, old
    village farmers
with nothing to do, hoes, plows, wooden rakes hung on
    brick walls
remembering the past

Lychee Grove

In fragrant lithe curves, the sun falls on the paulownia-
    covered hills
the lychee grove with its shadows and dark, inside its
    spacious
body the dusk shimmers, a cool brook plays a thousand-
    year-old
country melody—it can't adjust to the Industrial Age
it knows nothing of the hustle and bustle, it retains
an ancient slowness and sorrow, it lies like a sick patient
oily, dark, silted up with the stench of industrial waste
no one comes to listen to its low cries, on the hillocks
excavators uproot the lychees, the felled trees
topple onto the naked yellow earth, the delicate flowers
fall, the fragrance fades, here in the setting sun
I see Phoenix Avenue, how many of the people on it
have come from afar like me, to enjoy the prosperity of
    this Industrial Age
houses and radio towers spring up in the lychee grove I
    watched being felled,
the homes with Chinese dark-tiled roofs are replaced with
    a Western style
in this village, no one is like me
listening to what is behind the prosperity, the weeping
    brook and clear-cut
lychee trees in their grief, an old ancestral temple in a
    high-rise jungle

Stone Anchor

I've met with expansive sorrow, impressive as the open sea
a bright flickering ache halting inside a tiny needle hole

Crash—wham, for all these years, I've been banging away
    between sorrow and joy
being creative, amid all these incalculable human lives,
    these multitudes
of human emotions

I am the stone anchor of fate, *crash—wham*, putting
    everything aside
and pinning it down

To Give

I've endured the fading away of gentle youth
for many years life has been
like a dulled word I've been revising
I try to study love, hate, forgetting
old desires grow weathered, get stranded
old angers are rubbed smooth by time, are lost,
leaving behind an empty name, let the thin
pen collect it, these years, I've tried
to be someone pure, writing poems, studying,
but the smoke of reality chokes me
the injured fingers, unemployment, poverty, illness
they've altered me, I live in perplexity
turned melancholy by distant events
used up by drudgery, allowing a few words
to suffuse my life, like disgrace, grief,
loneliness—but there is a quieter word too: poetry

Language

I speak this sharp-edged, oiled language
of cast iron—the language of silent workers
a language of tightened screws   the crimping and memo-
    ries of iron sheets
a language like calluses   fierce   crying   unlucky
hurting   hungry language   back pay of the machines' roar
    occupational diseases
language of severed fingers   life's foundational language in
    the dark place of unemployment
between the damp steel bars   these sad languages

...........I speak them softly

in the roar of the machines. A dark language. Language of
    sweat. Rusty language
like a young woman worker's helpless eyes or an injured
    male worker by the factory doors
their hurting language   language of shivering bodies
language of denied compensation for injured fingers

Rust-speckled switches, stations, laws, the system. I speak
    a black-blooded fired language
of status, age, disease, finances...a fearful, howling
    language. Tax collectors and petty officials.
Factory bosses. Temporary residence permits. Migrant
    workers...their languages
language of a girl jumping off a building. The GDP's
    language. Language of official projects. Language of a
    kid's school fees.

I speak of stone. Of overtime. Violent language
I speak of . . . the abyss. Climbing the ladder. Unreachable
　　distances
the language of holding life's railings in the gusts of
　　fruitless labor

I speak—

these sharp-edged oiled languages, their pointy edges open up
to stab this soft era!

A Needle Hole Through the Constellations

A needle hole through the constellations, a safety alarm
    like a crow at dusk
cawing from atop a steel-needled sewing machine, moon-
    light partitioned
by gaslight, the skin of a quarter of its light and shadow
burned by the acid bath, a rust cleanser purging day and
    night
from the deep recesses of the sun iron, rib of industry,
    fondles
the injured city. Under the cutting machine, existence
cracks, fades, refuses to compromise.

Afternoon follows the screw threads' steady motion
wedging into the marsh of evening, and the rickety moon
is a patient with an occupational disease, gasping in the
    haze. An ultrasonic wave
undulates and descends, like a tireless loquacious singer
knowing nothing of humor, drowsiness crawling up from
    the machine
to fall on my eyelashes, the green indicator flashing
the mechanical arm pulls from the electroplated sink
    bundles of bright shiny
dawns. Life passes on a pulley, elapsing,
sinking into an industrial cesspool.

The machine starter sinks rapidly into the acid bath, the
    night throws off
its dark clothing. Moonlight, night's safety alarm,
begins to shine, the snow finally stops falling. Electroplating
    solution seeps out

in thick smoke and foam, each iron sheet between death
    and birth
hurts, becomes hesitant and weary, they're stuffed into
the heat treatment tank, the moon absconds from the
    enormous container
of the sky. Life imprisoned between sky and earth, like
    iron
in the heat treatment tank, hardening.

Woman Worker (2012)

Woman Worker
Youth Pinned to a Station

Time opens its enormous maw the moon on the machine
rusting   tired   darkened   turbid   its inner danger
gurgles past   the cliff of the body collapses   into mud and
    splintered stones
the splinters of time   turbulent waters fill a woman's body
wild tidal waters no longer fluctuating with the seasons
    she sits at her station
the flowing products and interlocking time   are swallowed
    up   quickly
aging   ten years flowing past like water   enormous
    weariness
floats through the mind   for many years   she's stuck by
the screws   one screw   two screws   turning to the left
    to the right
fixing her dreams and her youth to some product   look
at her pale youth   running   from an inland village
to a factory by the sea   all the way to a shelf in America
fatigue and occupational diseases build up in the lungs
get caught in the throat   a lifetime of irregular periods
fierce coughing   the distant development zone of factories
the clear-cut green lychee trees   the machines by her side
shivering   she rubs her swollen red eyes   and sticks
    herself back
into the flow of products

Zhou Hong

You tell me of your illusory and unstable life
fate is like a tired vehicle   turning towards the body's cold
unexpected reality stabs you   fallen angels
or streetwalkers at night   red neon and dubious shadows
beauty shops or dressing rooms   signs for snack shops
lit-up hotels   pink beds...
grief gathers like sediment in the busyness   silence   a
     lonely but happy
life   carrying the faint odor of a fallen woman   those
     words *fallen woman*
are a bit too much   beautifully seductive   a sexy angel
flesh and flirtatious glances   it was 1997   seventeen years
     old
in a grimy hair salon somewhere in Guangdong   a black
     sofa
dark trees   hazy sun alights on the changing street
yes   your companion tells me how clumsy you were back
     then
sitting in an unfamiliar town   depressed from your first
     time away from home   but now
that's all in the past   in a yellowing picture by the seaside
     your smile is young
as though witnessing something   including your youth
you're not ashamed   of any of it   just slightly regretful
2001   you'd had four abortions   an ache in your abdomen
the third time was with a so-called boyfriend   once you
     didn't know whose it was
it left behind   indistinct clots that had to be
scooped out of your body   you seemed unburdened   you
     had seen

the scraping and flushing of the one-child policy   it was
    just ordinary
surgery   2003 a gynecological disease   2004 in Changsha,
    Hunan
in some small hotel along Highway 107   you sold yourself
    to the drivers passing through
your flesh   2005 you tried to return to a normal path
    eight years
of a fallen woman's life   you were weary   tired of it all
marriage meant a village twenty kilometers from home
    a decent man
no one mentions your past   no one wants to mention it
these days   in China's remote villages   so many girls
share your fate   selling their bodies in unfamiliar places
returning home as daughters   wives   mothers   in 2006
you returned to the role of a loyal wife   went back with
    your husband to Panyu, Guangdong
he worked in a car garage   you worked in a grocery store
renting in a slum   full of dreams for the future   a year
    into the marriage
you still hadn't conceived   your in-laws nagged   your
    husband is their only child
by 2007 you'd tried Chinese and Western medicine   your
    grandmother
visited a witch doctor   and you finally conceived
and miscarried   in 2008 another ectopic pregnancy
and in the end it knocks you to pieces   in 2010   amid
    fights and
abuse you finally divorced   you went back to that hotel
    on Highway 107
six months later   no one knew where you'd gone...

Liu Meili

At seventeen she   was like a simple electrical component
plugged into life's circuit board   the future
was a whirlpool of uncertainty   full of confusion and danger
her gentle nature could temper the mire of life
just as her smile held an unshakeable happiness
she turned screws   welded semiconductor chips   her large
    eyes
sparkling with a hopeful glow   under the fluorescent lights
she fumbled among the products   the cold wound of time
there was a secret force building up in her body
the assembly line machinery moved like her
clumsily   she loved the view
of the somewhat dim lives of the migrant workers
she plugged in components   between blue wires
a fine copper wire   threaded itself from the assembly line
into her village soul   wages of a thousand kuai
couldn't satisfy her young heart   she was used to saving
one hundred and fifty kuai extra a month made her feel rich
she sent her wages back to her Hunan village   she became
the model of a woman who'd left to find work   the
    calluses on her fingers
were like a river revived   carrying along her eight years
of loneliness   her only plan was to return to her village
    and marry

Li Juan

An open-air reality   the theater of life contains
hard labor and sorrow   cold plotting and moods
increasing duties and achievements   drudgery
becomes a footnote to fate   the swallows head south
flying high and low   from here to there   giving her
confusing signs   from electronics factory to toy factory
she is an unaccomplished rivet
from village to factory   she hasn't yet shed
her life's undertone   and that becomes
her best explanation   changes of factory   changes
of hairstyle   changes of boyfriend   changes of
future plans   she's like a hopping frog
always taking a leap   on urban paved streets
that she can't get used to   she wants to evolve into
a frog who can live in a jungle of steel bars
she wants to escape a traditional fate   leaving home at
    eighteen
she's like a tree transplanted in the city   she has to put
    down roots fast
or else she'll return to her village   and relive the life of a
    previous generation
she moves from the electronics factory to the hardware
    factory
reality is not
nearly as nice as she'd imagined   smaller factories have
    fewer people
who are easier to deal with   big factories offer more
    opportunities...
she hasn't yet managed to cast off her assembly line fate
from Jiangxi to Dongguan   three years   twenty-one

years old   her family urges her to come back at New Years
    to find a husband
she wants out of the family   confines but fears
her future will be dim   her youth is fading
older women have trouble getting married   she struggles
    with indecision
go back and find a husband   or look for better opportunities
she wants a reason not to find a husband
so she jumps again   like a frog on cement
leaping   the hot cement will scorch her

Shu Miao

As for reality   you and I are the same   we never
begrudge it   we both need gratitude   and as for
fate   whether bumpy or smooth
we both respect it   and we haven't lived
too badly   a thousand-kuai salary for example
an eleven-hour workday   you can handle
the present situation   often
waiting for that rare vacation   payday   stroll
to buy cheap pretty clothing   your smile
is infectious   for you life is
light and gentle   you don't worry about economics
the law   wealth disparity   factories promising room and
    board
but have no concept of three meals a day
you prefer your MP3s   Jay Chou's singing   online gaming
QQ chats   pretty cross-stitch embroidery   while the fight
    to vote
the economic crisis   exist in a distant world
product quantities   inferior products   mechanical failures
overtime   a raise   for you that's everything
or saving whatever you can save of your wages
no matter what   you're still stuck on
"after all, being a migrant worker is easier than staying at
    home and farming...
at least there's a future here"   "after all, the factory pays
    us on time
and won't withhold wages"   "after all, more orders means
    we have jobs'
"the factory dormitories aren't that bad, after all"
"after all..."   behind those millions of *after alls*
I see millions of simple hearts   they belong

mostly to women workers in China   *after all* doesn't come from
   self-deception   but from the soul   as for fate
the one worry   is about going home at New Years to find
   a husband
all of your hope rests on finding a good man
since after all it matters for the rest of a woman's life

Kneeling Workers Demanding Their Pay

The women flash by like ghosts   at bus stops
machine stations   industrial zones   filthy rented rooms
their thin bodies   like razor blades   like white paper
like strands of hair   like the air   they use their fingers to
     slice
iron   film   plastics   their exhausted numb
faces are like ghosts   they're installed in machine stations
work uniforms   assembly lines   their bright gazes
young ages   they hide in their self-constructed
dark tidal currents   I can't tell them apart anymore
just like no one can tell me apart from them   leftover
     leathery
bodies   motion   blurred faces   one after another
innocent faces   they're constantly put together   arranged
into an electronics factory ants nest   a toy factory hive
     they
laugh   stand   kneel   bend   huddle
they've been simplified down to fingers   and thighs
they've become tightened screws   sliced iron sheets
compressed plastic   bent aluminum wire   cut cloth
their expressions   of disappointment   pride   exhaustion
     happiness
chaos   helplessness   loneliness
they come from villages   hamlets   valleys   neighbourhoods
     they're smart
clumsy   timid   weak
today they kneel   facing the big bright window
the black-uniformed guards   the lustrous cars   the green
     bushes
the factory sign shines bright in the sun
they kneel at the factory entrance   holding a cardboard sign

with the scrawled words   *Give us our hard-earned money*
the four women kneel in the factory entrance without fear
the onlookers around them   a few days ago   were village
    acquaintances
co-workers   friends or   working the same machines
they watch the kneeling women impassively
they witness their four co-workers dragged off by the
    guards   they witness
one of the worker's shoes falling off   they witness another
    worker's
pants ripped in the struggle   they watch silently
as the four workers are dragged somewhere far away   their
    eyes
hold no sorrow and   no pleasure   they impassively enter
    the factory
and their misfortune depresses me no end

Zhang Ai

You're full of petty bourgeois feelings   pledging loyalty to
    perfume
bar alleys   Japanese manga   whisky or rock'n'roll
travel   smoky eye makeup   years like the skin must be
    kept moisturized
Chinese-style jackets and cocktails   giving those dull
    working days
a little fun   in black fingernail polish
the future is exchanged for credit   the past doesn't have
    time to swipe its card
you go to the disco without a backwards glance   everything
    at high speed
rocking away your time   a spider tattooed on your leg and
a butterfly on your stomach   opens its beautiful wings
you are used to pretending   the lies spread like weeds
enjoyment is a lifestyle choice   you want to
just drift along   different faces for different places
sometimes you suspect   that actually
frugality is a kind of luxury   you are always fixing
your life   your rural identity
a clerk at a hardware factory   the dull numbers and iron
    plating
compose your face   rusted youth
not much is left   it's starting to fade   though still stitched
with a young girl's borders   your future is still only
    imaginary
a fate thinner than paper   you need lipstick
thicker silk stockings   older co-workers
poke their heads out of numbers   too much fakery and
    depression
not content with a traditional life   they stick their heads

into the sand of statistical reports   file folders and office
    buildings blue uniforms
stretching out into pure white scandals   her thighs and the
    boss
enough nerve and capital   to change one's fate
it's hard to avoid rhetorical versions   "to marry
a rich man" probably does take some tricks and artifice
you begin to calculate which buttons to push   quality is
    itself
only a show   people laugh at you for aiming too high
you don't mind   you don't give up on yourself
cafés and beauty shops   tattooed eyebrows full of sweetness
love is reduced to economic exchange   too much
    imagination lives in these
sitting in time's tin shack   your third relationship is
    already done for
the next one is turning down the street   looking for a
    warehouse affair

Ding Min

We're not daydreaming kids anymore   reality took all
your dreams and crushed them   leaving iron nails   work-
    stations   plastic film filling up
our fates   they laugh at us like defective goods
our useless lives   our labor deconstructed
by redone work   reality is a mechanical hand jutting from
    a workstation
holding down everything we dreamed of   and so idealism
    dies of thirst
like the moon running dry   illuminating the oily
    workstations
these past few years   sickness has taken root in your frail
    body nosebleeds
colds   you seem like an emaciated moon   sometimes I
    worry
whether your seventy-something-pound frame can support
    a single iron nail
you use shy laughter and dry numbers to prove
from 2004 to today   you worked hard at night school
    distance learning
or Japanese classes   you grow tired of a rootless life
but our lives are destined to float through this world
we make restless attempts to settle down   only to return
    to restlessness
you lost your mother when you were five   "Mother's gone
    far away"
many years ago   your mother's spare shadow
became a memory of a faraway place   unhealing
wounds   like pins stuck in your body   stabbing you
your mother is caught in a five-year-old's haze   immense
    and blurred

indistinct lives and memories   "life is damp as mist"
"you can't let yourself get lost in the mist"   you said to me
the mists of the Hunan countryside   gather the dust of time
to torment you   your pain is so bright
it pierces your thin body   "you can only depend on your-
    self"
you're determined   over these many years   you've kept
    trying
enduring   "don't ever let yourself cry"

Yan Fen

Rejecting clarity   you don't want to seek out
truth   or rip life to bloody shreds
what's the point of making things heavy and sad
I'm always thinking of pain   dark words
"why does life have to be so exhausting   what can we
    change anyway"
you say to me   but all I've ever known
is heaviness itself   I still have enough patience
and anger at reality   perhaps one day I'll be like you
exhausted   with no love for the world and no anger either
just life itself   until death covers over everything
for so many years   we've been worn down
Little Fen went to Shenzhen to sell her body   Wei Qi
    married someone in Henan
Zheng Mei went back home   Xu Hui died in a car wreck
you often say   "heaven knows   perhaps one day
I'll die in some accident"   "that's real life
that's our fate   we're all doomed to end up back home"
whether I describe it or not   what was meant to pass has
    passed
what is meant to come will come   these melancholy words
can't free us from our troubles they can't
redress a betrayed marriage   they can't rescue and redeem
our inner selves   reality has taught us just more insipid
realism   only memory soothes the youth that once was
    ours
it leaves tears and pleasure for our rootless lives
and sorrow and happiness   we remember the buses we took
to the sheet-iron shacks of Gaoying Village   security
    teams   the Konka Furniture factory
the train of time whistles past   an entire decade

when we meet up again   in a small restaurant to reminisce
about your two failed marriages   my staying single
time sifts us out at different angles
until finally we drown in the past   I use pointless poems
to remember your lot or mine over the past decade
it seems the black-and-white rolls of silent film   have
    finally faded
these years   your destiny of drudgery   marriage
children   crow's feet   neither of us is able
to see life clearly   it brushes past us
leaving behind real but illusory memories   like the gleam
    of streetlamps in the dusk

Xiong Man

Toiling in the rain   blown by the wind
off-kilter   staggering   a mother's heart
crushed   on the phone she talks with her eight-year-old son
at her son's tears her empty heart
is emptied further   "I'll come home at New Years
be good and listen to Grandpa and Grandma"   with her
    sick elderly father
she discusses   the crops the rice paddies   village gossip
the summer mosquitoes   the willows felled from the
    riverbank
the rain falls from Guangdong to Hunan
a thick drizzle   gentle   from industrial Guangdong
to touch the impoverished Hunan countryside   all night
    long the rain
carries a mother's heart a   heart of leaving
an aching heart   a gleam of young eyes in the rain
rain of an unfamiliar place   like piano keys being pressed
    in a grey
industrial area and in the distant countryside   chiming
    notes
two hearts of leaving meet each other in the rain's vast
    white
her son's cries never cease in the rain   she's thirty-two
a polisher in a hardware factory   the raindrops fall on the
    shiny iron plates
longing is everywhere like stains of rust   in the distant
    village
the young son and old father
the impoverished courtyard   broken roof tiles
the cries of a son left behind
seventeen years   and she's aged

the rain falls on the rooftops of Hunan   a distinct time
in her memory in the slow rain   the youth she has left
is collected by the raindrops   and narrated slowly
along the sky   such a muddy life   "go out into the world
and get a job   we'll take care of Little Sheng"   son and
    daughter-in-law
at an electronics factory in distant Guangdong   grandson
    on his knees
at two years old the grandson cries "Mama" into the phone
his father died three years ago   and is buried in the earth
there is only this vast white rain   in the peaceful ground
they reincarnate   they chat in midair
like an ancient anonymous author   in a room at the back
    of the house
they talk about her life   a life of eighteen years of labor
she's aged   coming home   eighteen years later   she'll be
    buried too
her son will return home   only the rain gathers in the
    eaves and falls
where the water pools   like tears   like little round
hearts of leaving   splashing back up

Xu Rong

Life in its meaninglessness is given infinite fabricated
    meanings
even facing the dark failure of death
I maintain a glorious respect for life
Life   allows me to see miraculous things
I study the fate of these women   or of myself
bodies and souls riddled by industry   we
lose ourselves prematurely   dispersed into reality
leaving sickness   missing fingers   memories of a wounded
    surviving era
as I write these words   your pale face
reveals the frailty of your body   dizzy   heart palpitating
    breathing
labored   you slowly grow used to the Industrial Age
bringing the pain of illness   glue   benzene   combining in
    your veins
the worst isn't physical pain   social sickness
the countless women who share your fate   don't know
the cause of the sickness   returning from others' cities to
    their hometowns
enduring the torture of disease   quietly dying   becoming
    the silent section
industry shows its vanity in its own way
the society gets drunk on incomprehensible prosperity
    you drag
your feeble body   from the factory to the occupational
    diseases diagnosis center
to the environmental protection center   to the labor
    department you endure
the dual torture of social and physical sickness   medicine

flows through your veins   it grabs hold of illness's throat
   for a while
as social sickness continues to fester   from one kind of
   sickness
to another   it makes you see more clearly
other people's realities   yes   these illnesses make people
furious it turns people speechless   but you must
find the roots of the body's sickness   I see in your lonely
   eyes
the truest light there is already enough pain   we cannot
just blindly hurt   "so many people die without a diagnosis"
it's harder to navigate than rural Sichuan roads   we're all
   from Sichuan and feel our own fate
on the tortuous mountain roads   from "case not accepted"
   to "surgical tests of the lungs"
I am filled with uncontrollable pain and anger

Middle-Aged Prostitutes

Low tile-roof houses of the urban village   gloomy humid
    light
filthy mildewed sewers   they sit in the doorways
knitting sweaters   chatting   sizing up the men coming
    and going
their eye shadow and rouge can't hide their age
thirty or older   in the chaotic urban village
they talk about their business of the flesh and their
    customers
thirty kuai   twenty kuai   occasionally a customer
who pays fifty   they discuss the sweaters they're knitting
the patterns and colors   how they'll knit something for
    their distant
parents in Sichuan   or send the finished piece
to a distant son   their movements are agile
sometimes they discuss nearby colleagues who've been
    arrested
and fined four thousand kuai   they say each month they
    give three hundred kuai
to an insider   though this so-called protection fee
is ten times their normal fee   they say
it's like being crushed ten times by a devil   though this
    devil
is enormous but empty   they lose out
I imagine their current lives   and their former lives
and their future lives   as though under the sweaters
    they're knitting
is a mother's heart   a wife's heart and
a daughter's heart   they breathe in the dark and
moan helplessly after shutting the door   seen from behind
    they are

a bunch of mothers   sitting in a doorway knitting sweaters   these
    middle-aged prostitutes   with eyes like this country's face
just as uncertain   leaving us collectively confounded

Zhou Yangchun

In a dream world   she stands on a wharf
though there are no ships   or the test isn't over
the time has come   often it's defective goods   open and
    bleak
midnight in the mountains   her left alone   nothing to
    depend on
she told me what made her scream in the dream   lamplight
shining on her face after her screaming   relaxed and
    smooth
without daytime's silence and nervousness   in the dream
she had come across a deserted field   and had to cry out
    she was afraid
she screamed   and woke   next to twelve other people
in the cramped dorm room   her co-workers were shocked
she apologised   she said inside her body
was a hidden demon   that stayed curled up peacefully
    during the day
but at night emerging to torture her   her body still hadn't
    gotten used to it
working twelve hours a day in the electronics factory
    tired
became her only word   on the assembly line
her body stiffened and grew clumsy   joints hurting
her remaining fingers repeating motions like a machine
    her upper back
legs   lower back   she couldn't control them   strange pains
as though stones were crushing her body   she had to
    extract
a deserted field from her body   it made her scream   there
    was a beast
that escaped her sleep   this girl of seventeen from Hunan

screaming as though she were being crushed alive by
    stones   in her sleep
screams erupting from her flowing veins
penetrating the whole dorm   between her breathing and
    her screams
I felt in my insomnia a silent woman worker
her body teeming with pressure   her screams piercing
this cramped Industrial Age   like a battle cry
like something submerged in her turbulent veins
we complained that her screams broke
our good dreams her   innocent body and encompassing
    eyes
her screams in that dream became the slow anguish
inside the body of the Industrial Age   gathering   about to
    erupt

Child Laborers on Mt. Liang

Life is nothing if not bewildering   this era gradually turns
blind   a fourteen-year-old girl wants to come with us
pulling the exhaustion of these times towards her on the
    assembly line
sometimes   she wants to let herself return to her Sichuan
    village
chop firewood   cut grass   pick wild fruit and flowers
her small weak gaze reveals desolation   I don't know
how to describe it   I only know
child workers   are like sighs thin as paper
her gaze can smash a soft heart
why is it that what little sympathy exists
always gets crushed by the assembly line machines
her slow tempo is frequently answered
by the supervisor's abusive curses   she does not cry
her tears swim in her eyes   "I'm an adult
I don't cry" she says somberly
it's bewildering   what is left of youth is only
memory   she speaks of mountain things like hillsides
like bright blue ponds   like snakes   and cows
perhaps life is finding a path out of bewilderment
and back to itself   sometimes her dark face
reveals a look of contempt
and she points at another weaker girl and says
"She's younger than I am   but she's sleeping around"

Hu Zhimin

These days I'm immersed in this enormous era
I'm weak, powerless   smothering a vigorous life
in vast denial and ignorance
her death brought the era's wounds with it
along with men wrangling for compensation
her brothers and parents   her corpse ignored
no one grieved   no one wept
just the icy numbers of compensation to keep her company
Hu Zhimin: twenty-three years old   dead from alcohol
    poisoning
I have a clear memory of her
my one-time colleague   who was reduced to a hotel
prostitute   her innocent smile   loud talk
worldly experience   she told me she'd seen
too much of the so-called truth of life   standing
in the doorway to reality   such as desire and flesh
she wasn't too shy to discuss her profession
and her plans for life   in her town there were many
young women who took up the ancient profession
young newlyweds   sisters   sisters-in-law
going in together   to Nanjing   or down to Guangdong
in hair salons   gloomy buildings   she was quite pretty
in hotels   fancy places   a happy expression
on her face   we rarely met   we had
the same background   belonging to two
different worlds   this city   this moment
two people meeting and parting in life's arbitrariness
each hurrying off in her own direction
and was fate somehow changed   "she's dead!"
a man from her village told me   then described
how she died he said she sent so much money home

said her family home was expensive   her own brothers used
her body to make money   to buy a house in the village and open a shop
he said after she died   her brothers didn't even come
to bring her ashes home   she couldn't be buried in her family plot
she had sold her body   she was dirty   she'd ruin the fengshui of the family home

Moonlight
Married Workers Living Apart

Moonlight washes the steel faces, the moonlight leaves a
    line of footprints on the iron vines of the security wall
the moonlight lengthens the distance between buildings
    5 and 6, from the female dorm
to the male dorm, the moonlight stops in the window for
    a minute, the moon
illuminates him, or her
the moonlight illuminates their bodies, skeletons, inner
    desires, the moonlight illuminates
their memories of their wedding night, the moonlight is
    too bright
like salt poured into the wound of living apart eighteen
    days after their marriage

Moonlight illuminates the well in their bodies, illumi-
    nates the well of desire
the moonlight illuminates their fifteen-day honeymoon,
    illuminates his memory
of her body taken over by shade inch by inch, privet fruit
    trees
her body lies fallow in the moonlight, inch by inch
slipping along the forty-five meters between buildings
    5 and 6

If the moonlight were a bit closer, the expanse it's brought
    would be a bit bigger
her desire would be a bit deeper, if the moonlight were a
    bit darker
the wounds on her skin would be a bit wider, his inner
    torture would be
a bit deeper

Moonlight illuminates the unfinished building for married
    workers, the moonlight shines on an article in the paper
"The Sex Lives of Migrant Workers..."
if the moonlight were a bit darker, love would be a bit
    stronger
if the moonlight were a bit brighter, the future rooms for
    married couples would be a bit larger

Young Prostitutes

They sit cracking sunflower seeds in their teeth   playing
    mahjong
standing by the spicy soup vendor's cart
their delicate fingernails are covered in nail polish   they
    wear
silver jewelry or meditation beads   their naked arms
are printed with butterfly patterns   black low-waist shorts
rein in the passion of their rumps   blue eye shadow
shows disdain and confusion towards life   or
they sit idly in doorways talking   sometimes I pass by
their doorways   see their painted pale
faces   seductive faces   like a city or a country
decked out in high-rises   there's no way to peek beneath
    the rouge
at their paleness and fragility   their flashy dresses
hide diseased bodies and souls
for many years   I've passed by the government center
surrounded by prosperity   behind it are the slums
and struggling citizens   and with all this
I live amid deep apprehension

Woman Worker

The Patient Heart of Rural China

A cold greasy black stream of tears   hiding disease
in the veins   lungs stuffed with lead   your once clear eyes
are like another polluted stream   dazed and muddied
your emaciated body is like stars in a light-polluted sky
the bitterness of worn machinery   dismantled
    decomposed melted down
the caress of thin wages   ancient worries emerge between
    your eyebrows
five thousand years of shameful diseases   devour a
    dignified fate
your life follows simple country traditions
but today's laws can't be trusted   the protection of basic
    rights or lawsuits
is unimaginable   you have learned the same patience as
    our nation
power made the pigtail braids on men's heads
drag out for two hundred years   lung and blood diseases
the body's black weaknesses   at your obsolete workstation
    put in overtime
don't get paid on time   their black shadows harm you
in all of this   you use your rural Chinese heart for
    patience

Conversation

History is suctioned out, fabricated stories and extracts are
    put in its place
the confessions we want are collected by moonlight, in
    autumn
villages on the plains aren't scenic, stern as history
onerous truths, philosophy, art, it all wears me down
the train is passing by scattered towns and plains
outside the window, a few sparse stars at three a.m.
people wander through each other's dreams
time makes no sound as it moves, it is mysterious, reticent
in this oscillating distant place, I think of
those many faces worn down by history, they
leave behind so few fragments, like sparks
in the wilderness, illuminating an ice-cold distorted history

An Orange Decade

In the darkness we look for a luxurious dawn
but find instead a dogmatic revolution   its teeth
hold a nameless dread   violence from morning to night
blood and skulls mingle   it uses a bloodthirsty
brutal beauty to awaken a latent wildness
submitting over and over again to beastly cravings
worried heads secretly amass elegies and sorrow
hearts are hidden from view by violence   sympathy
    becomes heresy
or irresolution   it changes everything
decency and shame   between the orange rays of light
pity is like an abandoned city abandoned to the wilderness
    by the setting sun
it is forlorn   there is a bone-piercing ache

Moth

Our country is like a dream hung high in the dark
the people's dynasty is still in its pupa, I sink far
into the body's memory, the mountains and rivers tremble
in the moth's wings, if the wind blows it ruffles the people
    like feathers
in the wind resilient girls endure hunger and humiliation
the grass bends in the dusk's light between leaves
soaked in darkness, it turns around silently
over the water, flying backwards, between light blue flames
you're not a moth, but our country's fireworks will burn
    you up

Rose Courtyard (2016)

The World at Dusk

Memory suffuses the dusk, a girl weeping far from home
in the calm air in the back garden, time
is like a far-flowing afternoon river, smashed scales sparkle
youth cries out from the water, the autumn is sickly and
    depressed

Grandmother stands and cries with a bird arriving from the
    south
from the empty garden to the flowerpots sagging in the wind
the rose of fate, withered trees grow new bark
among those secluded here is Grandfather, drunk amid the
    hemp

He breathes low, piercing the rose-blossom autumn
the wind and trees moan, five girls, yearning for love,
with their faces powdered white,
feel their mortal desire gradually run dry

And I, at dusk decades later, write unconvincing lines
that nearly topple the courtyard's fate, in the light of
    evening
the twilit air fills adolescent girls with dreams
and the roses softly tell of faraway love

Wind beats day and night at the grey window lattice, dusk
    envelops
the declining courtyard, a beam illuminates a lonely,
    gloomy
desolation more lasting than a dream. The countryside is
    quiet
a pair of butterflies flit, crickets call low from the corner

No one will remember this bleak Rose Courtyard
its tranquil beauty hurts me, in this mortal afternoon
the past flows on like a river, and the five girls
who never met love are wretched in the wind

Myself

I must give up remembering Rose Courtyard, and return
to the real world, like giving up real tears in life
to put on a mask, and surrounded by the empty crowds
live, walk, hold out my hand to detestable people

Rose Courtyard, this tranquil castle, collects my
illusory youth, the wind sees off the autumn, by fine stone
    paths
roses open, the insects drone, startled birds take flight
amid leaves just turning red, the bright calm dusk

White wings flap on and on, long thin feet stretch taut
the fading shadows hurt me, roses and poetry
soothe my wounds, more potent than opium
and in the mystical courtyard, my body is drenched in
    peace

Autumnal winds stir the bleak courtyard, the birds on
    branches
sing, the water clings to dull rocks, autumn roses
slowly sway, and everything exists in ripeness and death
five thin shadows follow the wind through the paneled
    door

I return to the courtyard, carrying three damp books
and feminist thoughts unsuited to the time
longing for the old days of the courtyard, the five grand-
    mothers
with their love and disparate fortunes

Twilight envelops the courtyard, day and night replace
    success and failure
the sadness of fallen flowers on autumn days, a bird of love
and beyond, these thoughts are entangled with time
I give my soul to its carrying cry

Needlework

Soft hands stroke the embroidered pillow of grass-hued
    smoke
the needlework exudes the must of time, Grandmother
sews fate and love into the quilt of fiction
whose warmth holds no memory of excitement or passion

The strange dreams of a girl, more than sixty years later
harken back to olden times, rouge, fine jade, wood carvings
the back wing in the courtyard's shadow and the grand-
    mothers
smell of the past, like her own ensnarled heart

It holds a Chinese woman's entire lifetime
she once looked on love with hope
the silken past, cloth shoes spotted with tears
full of metaphors and desolation that must not be divulged

Faced with time and memories more tangled than her
    needlework
she uses colored silk to weave a pattern of love and fate
the moon glitters, illuminating the silks and satins of the
    flowers
a nightbird startles into flight, its call mild and low

The lamp illuminates the flower petals, the evening
    breezes dry the dew
memories set fire to the past, a wounded elegant love
rain soaks into the heart, it follows the needle's footsteps
to weave the mournful Sichuan brocade of Rose Courtyard

Fallen petals coat the path, the back wing's cold air presses in
autumnal roses blossom on Grandmother's face, her needle-
   work
swarms with confusion, she uses a plaintive needle
and despairing thread to embroider a Rose Courtyard
   autumn

Illness

Each day is longer than the last, the blood slows in the body
rain clouds press down overhead, youth withers, your
    frailty
and careful but hasty breath, in the clear winter
the trees are spotless, time once again rejects

The liquid parts of your body, and you turn stiff
will the body continue to be as it was, like a billowing silk
    sleeve
soft, fully refined, waves roving towards the banks
withered cane clings to the corners, the protagonist's
    lifelong spell

On ruined winter days, carved wood eaves anchor the quiet
inflammation and pain. The idle dressing table
deep within the dreamworld of the past, returns to the
    cold heart
the bones' fragrance and frigidity, and time gathers up

Your sins of your heart, the deep fog of your misfortune
a sentimental drama, a beauty among beauties
the smell of decay spreads everywhere, seeping from the
    body
amid loneliness and rust, you cannot sing your sorrow

Not avoiding blushes and heartbeats, the days wriggle
    their thin waists
the Suzhou Canal shrinks in the cold winter countryside
too far from Sichuan, the heart is like a long river corridor
with dark green waterweeds and secrets like sap from a
    stalk

Illness, coughing, the south takes root in the body
washes the snow and sorrow from the throat, worries like
    trees
cover the body, and time has no direction
there is only illness spreading weakness and misfortune

Sparrow

The dark sweet voice of opium awakes, dimming the back
  wing's
mute farmer. Iron hoe. Plum trees. The sparrow opens its
  mouth and bends
towards the flowers, in northern gloom, a slightly bitter
  sparrow
flies low over the roses, and the garret that stores the play
  of youth

Desolate winter, the sparrow is like a container of insect
  dramas
or like grey silverware, its bright spots' soft fate
it takes flight, the scent of the garden drifts about
its sharp mouth pecks a snowdrift, grey belly pressed to a
  plum tree branch

In the back garden, it's like a grey note, its high call
and inhibited rhythm, in the snow the mute farmer sees
  fate's
withered branches, on the black window lattice, shuttling
  back and forth
like a burning dance, the north wind stirs his mute life

He becomes a Kunqu opera scene, *falling leaves startle the
  unfinished dream
everything is given to destruction*, the snow covers the
  path
he digs flower roots and flames out of the petalled mud, in
  the sparrow's
flying shadow, the dusk wanes, the withered branches still

Withered branches. Sparrow. These metaphors, sugges-
    tions in the snow
spherical eye sockets with tears and light, boiling notes
the mute farmer's throat convulses with soundless voice,
    expanding and contracting
like a trapped sparrow, suddenly flapping its wings but
    unable to fly
The sparrows perch, snow drifts to the ground, they throw
    their shadows
against the mute farmer's pupils, the plum tree branches
    in the back garden
pistils like palace maids, the only warm thing in the
    courtyard
absorbs the snow's glow, a tender stomach meeting a
    tender flame

Foreign Land

Horses or lanterns on paper, blood or music in the body
silk petals wither, time gallops towards Yunnan
your paltry body rushes across the country, with your
yearning, passion, duty becoming testimony to an epoch

For years, I've felt the bone-chill of war
your bodies are like lamps warming our country
so many years later, I read your letters by the courtyard's
    light
and a heart full of passion leaps from the paper

"Weak and thin, with a pair of bright eyes," Grandmother
    says of you
"In the midst of despair is the beat of flames," you wrote
I read of brutal war more than seventy years ago in the
    history books
eight years of massacres, the sun and moon and stars...
    other nouns as well

"Don't worry about me," your letter begins
I imagine subtropical jungles, beasts, and sickness
loneliness and hunger, life and death, roses and guns
homesickness, light like black juice and unruffled officers

These unfamiliar words choke my throat like smoke
subtropical plants and their sharp odors
I cannot touch you, my relative, buried in a foreign land
a medal from the war of resistance becomes proof of a
    tragic era

Recently, I've seen news about your comrades in battle
and dreamed of that jungle, where my relative is buried
I live in lethargy, writing poetry, watching my loved ones
    decline
thinking in the exhausted dusk, "Don't worry about me."

Setting Sun

He stands between two trees and his narrow shadow
    flickers
this hardworking mute farmer, the windows hold the
    sunset, clouds burn across the sky
birds return to their home in the eaves, twilight accumu-
    lates sadness, green leaves get lost
at dusk, his heart is like a withered tree, forlorn

Everything is grieving, youth, the lamplight, the pickaxes
in the back garden, a dispirited darkness and springtime
    grow, gurgling
water, hesitant seasons, he grows roses and sleeps
amid cherry trees and fatigue, turning to glimpse the
    night, the passage

Of bashful uncertainty, the flowers are too showy, he's too
    thin, too dark
the setting sun paints a mottled pattern on his face, the
    green
steps float with fallen flowers and stillness, he isn't sad, nor
inconstant, he uses silence to test the depths of the
    world's chaos

He fertilizes the flowers and plucks off insects, birds are
    above, fish
are in the water, in the night sky he sees stars, but destiny
    doesn't glitter
and the setting sun isn't sad, in the foliage are spiders,
    under the trees
are toads, the distance is tired, he uses shears

To prune spring and summer, autumn and winter, plants
    and the east wind, rain-filled
clouds have his tragic face, and I meet with a nameless
    suffering
the abandoned garden is unfamiliar and mild, window
    lattices are heaped with last year's colors
and the five grandmothers' liquid loneliness, I eavesdrop
    from the back wing

In a weak dusk, reflections of green trees and red flowers
    in the well
the beauty of late spring, and under the grandmothers'
    windows are customs and
silk clothing, traces of frost and tears, the mute farmer's
    flute is gentle
and the setting sun sighs outside, apart from loved ones,
    far apart

Rain

The thin heart melts willow trees and pine colors, outside
    is the sound of rain
someone knocks and lights the lamp, someone screams
    from a dream, the night
caves down into a staircase, who is climbing the stairs,
    who spirals up
blue sky as the rain lifts and clouds reform, people walk
    beyond the walls

Who does he wait for, as a fine rain wets the heart, a red
    candle and a cold lonely bed
the cape jasmine holds tears, roses drape across the east
    wind, rain outside
pacing the courtyard, she listens to the rain, the aged sky
distorts beyond recognition, exhausted clouds walk their
    arduous path

The rain extends with the staircase, wetting her ears,
    bringing
mists and clusters of stars, gathering autumn and familiar
    footsteps from chrysanthemums
last year stands outside the garden, rain pounds the young
    willows, caws come
in an old dream, bats prick the eaves, and I in my ancestral
    home light the lamp and read

Cold mist in the courtyard, scattered lamps in empty
    windows, the grandmothers tell stories with rain
their voices are far off, it's drizzling and chilly, I write
    poems

drink wine, listen to the wind, research the red lacquer
    furniture and carved antique armchairs
the past has a tail like stars, and who still waits now, the
    rain unceasing

Everything has changed, they disappear into the bamboo
    forest
I write about the clothes of yesteryear, Grandfather's
    illness envelops him
the grandmothers are peaceful and affectionate, their best
    years like running water, thinking
of loss spreading across their bodies, opening the door to
    cold rain, fallen leaves, dark clouds

Someone coughs in the rain, he married off his time to
    opium and illness
customs castigate seasons and tears, despise the pine
    colors and bamboo forest
my poems find the thwarted roof, its slow loneliness
spreads across the garret, the rain sinks into the body of
    my ancestral home, without sound

Finale

In the Hardware Factory

God's lazy too and produced humans on an assembly line
I could find my other half anywhere
they're as standardized as goods made in a factory,
a marriage gives rise to thorns of resentment, from noon
    to sunset
you live among the thorns, the pain is hard to bear,
    thinking of the pretty girl in the mirror
thinking of bone diseases, thinking of the conventions of
    Chinese medicine
you hear death's name, and it's like a piece of steel
inlaid in your bones, you can't afford to be sick,
a butterfly flapping its wings inside a three-thousand-
    degree boiler
you'll think it was a beast in a past life
running across an African savanna, but your disease
    started with the beast
of a machine, from levers to screws, from blueprints to
    callipers
from loneliness to a lost youth, it smells of hardware
    factory tools
and you're nothing but a lump of iron, thinking of words
    involving iron
like sheen, iron oxide, cast iron, steel, thinking of its
    sharpness
and the pain it causes as it pricks the body, thinking of its
    enormous
spindles, pulverising dreams into powder, thinking of its
    steel needle
sewing up a wound, if needed
starting out from love in the labor laws, smearing bread
    with butter

in hope, these night-time machines at 11:14 p.m.

these thoughts wriggle like fish, she huddles between the
    callipers

and there is a different world outside, with its songs of
    debauchery

A lion would have trouble reaching the tip of steel's
    thinking

a steel monster has her by the throat, and in its bones

are violent rain and thunder, heartfelt fantasies, and the
    iron turns from black to red

turns cold and grey like frost in my stomach

or it installs itself in the gears or levers or pulleys of this
    moment

we need an energy-saving era, but all the inferior goods

are turned into a symbol of iron by my forsaken organs, it
    was once

a nostalgic spring equinox, stove fires lighting up the
    many metaphors and symbols

you made certain genitals out of iron, made them hard

Chinese medicine originated with the moon, waxing and
    waning

you cut patterns of a cross, a sun, a penis at your cutting
    machine

and the thunder brings silver wings across the sky, steel
    has its own

mouth and taste, one must use sliding callipers or a
    compass to calibrate

the hunger of an epoch, the officials are anxious to learn,
    the poor have grown used to crying

the countryside has learned to pollute, the cities are being
    demolished, torn down, dismantled

our dispirited bodies feel the future struggling to take shape

his designs depart from realism, Romantics

start to feed on illusion, our futures get better and better, just keep on

signing contracts of truth with blind men, he imagines plums

on the southern mountains, he tells us that the eggs in his hands are rocks

time seems set apart, from the Four Modernizations of the '80s

I still haven't made it to the twenty-first century's low slope of prosperity

the mountains are still so high, but the body rots, and how many years will it take

to reach utopia, I pity myself as I age

unable to squeeze onto communism's last train

instead living in a scorching workshop in a sweat and blood factory,

like an autumn cicada about to cast off its shell, unnameable, unsummonable, unable

to traverse a time of credit, the sunlight of ideals, a dim silent future

there's no time for the machine-cut trash piled beside the new century

the first stage of socialism is over, time begins to recant

it laughs at our memories and enthusiasm as they slip away, you keep up your praise

nothing can absorb more than empty time

I long for the past, twenty years of a turned loom spins a classical thread

the needle of the Great Leap Forward sewed the clothes of reform and opening up,

the bureaucrats' livers darken, and they're shady enough already

so much worth seeing has been destroyed, what's left is an unbroken eulogy these goddamn soft bones, he always planned to use

the wings of lies to walk on the moon, the poor man, so
    servile

I'm accustomed to breaking iron, polishing it, drilling holes,
    creating the exterior

of this era, I arrange my fate on a piece of ironware

swimming alone in tears of iron, inserting my body into
    iron

letting it carry me to some faraway place, this hardship is
    life's

grand banquet, where one must use worry for wine and
    penurious food

what does this world have to offer me aside from worries,
    what else

can console us, living such difficult lives...

The reality is princes and party bosses, tax collectors and
    the political system, on rainy days

they hold meetings to discuss the country's yin and yang,
    the roads, ideology, how there's a need

for more email attachments and ordinances, how trees need
    steel altars, how the moon will be reborn

in water, a surmise deserves praise, its bewitching password
    comes from Tomb Sweeping Day

ancestral supernatural powers, its cheekbones are too high,
    her fate is too terrible, her poetry

is too good, the craving for leftover iron is too hard and
    stabs into this soft epoch

in her last life she was a phoenix, reborn as a lion, the steel
    is too dark

the isms too many, leaving her shapely body to surrender to
    the world, interact with the night

appearing, intersecting, coinciding, and they have identical
    faces

it already can't return to the prairie, its definition is
    expanding, extending
the leftover seeds from Grain Rain Day bring you good luck
morality is fragile, its body is skewered on steel shame-
    lessness, the spiders spin webs
the moths leap to flame, I can't avoid the tall building's
    tilt, its arrogant expression
the naturalists' lingering warmth feels good but loses
    confidence
it is still sunk in the self-pitying elegant scenery of the
    past, she comes from the Sichuan countryside
the hometown of milkvetch, returning from forests to
    steel, a bleak heart fills with ivy
polishing poems amid machines, moulding it with iron
    and blueprints, life is
this toil, the burning heat of the hardware workshop,
    electric saws and steel hammers, the sago palms on the
    windowsill, the palms outside
traditional wood, they're formed into frames, strips,
    shapes, like ancient doctrines
you hold tight to Japanese silk roses, German gears,
    imitation callipers, it's tragic, this imitation factory
starts to produce counterfeit boxes and lids, like coffin
    after coffin, filled with my soul
they're independent from your body and soul, they hold
    endless secrets
the draftsmen sink into lines, the moulders craft by
    appearance,
statisticians compute numbers, bosses calculate profits,
    while I do overtime overnight
and the moon in the window only lights up my dreams,
    the quality inspector stamps in red
signs her name and number, I face the cold steel and the
    unresponsive vastness

memory lies in waste like a development zone, gazing at
    an ancient temple encircled by factories
old-fashioned, deserted like ruins, like an archaeological
    site, *the air trembles with the scent of hemp*
I write this line on the back of graph paper, and the
    trembling will transfer
from paper to flesh, if I still need to explain, I got used to
    abstractions and comfortable seats with the production
    supervisor
she has a tongue like fine iron wire, twisting around order
    forms and customers, the overhead lights
illuminate my doctrines and notations, face-to-face with
    iron pincers and knives, she flips a switch
and turns on disease, and the iron on the machine is
    polished, rounded, squared, corrugated, to the left
or to the right, I'm a good citizen, the gears catch as they
    turn, and the iron bars turn
into toys, VCDs, the silent iron will be given a rare long
    journey
the thread-cutter thrusts out a crablike pincer, grabbing
    onto Confucius's poetry, thoughts, and profits,
grains of life's original quiet, lifting towards the shady
    places with the production supervisor's skirt, and all
    night the lamp
lights up a blueprint for the future, these threads are fairly
    simple, these doctrines have some mistakes
I open the valve to life, this postmodern art, what do
    springtime's dark ghosts need
the iron is forged, its wet silhouette blooms in the iron
    webbing, it wears
a dark iron coat, wears a dark iron scarf, you look up at
    the clock at the top of the church
now my blood pressure skyrockets, it rises with our
    collective shame

for so many years, I couldn't ford the river of isms, politics'
    swimming champions grow
scales, the bell's clang lives on in time, while time is so
    long and life is so short
what's left of the city lacks education, it tries to start a
    red-light district, big hotels
raise bright mosaics, it's a shame the old holdouts don't
    understand a harmonious society
these defective kids and flashy products, the strange odor
    filling my life
will they come into bloom, will they wither and fall, look
    at the workshop's polisher
who starts to stick out a reformed finger, life is a
    transaction, her back is to a rock's
cold heart, overtime in a sweat and blood factory has
    destroyed my heart, I'm like a prisoner
who's given up freedom for a new life, there are still three
    processes left, rivet joints,
soldering, and isn't it like a beast biting into you, iron
    shavings flying,
with so many nightmares, we need someone to warm our sleep

As soon as I could I left this life of iron, it practiced a kind
    of Romanticism
on the machines, pulled dreams out of the last drilled hole,
    left behind a hundred shapes
and a hundred futures, as I bear loneliness in the shrieks of
    iron, it carved
my registration, age, file, temporary residence permit on a
    drill bit, it records
my work number and jobs, it forges prisoners' cages, uses
    production numbers to track
our emotional states, its blueprints are twilight theories,
    requiring philosophy and political theory

iron is delivering a speech on the machines, it's waiting
    for the name of a theory or a style
I'm already used to magical realism, worshipping the
    mute, now it's perfect
for a kind of opening up, from ore to iron, from iron to
    products, this is
the process of iron establishing a political party, it uses
    callipers, blueprints, switches, and
of course electricity, those words you softly muttered, like
    water
flowing through your nerves, you tremble as you recite
    electricity, iron turns electricity
into party regulations and power, these collective parties
    of iron tools start to tell me what to do
drill holes here, fold there, it speaks in translation, good at
    guarding against
the mixed grief and confusion of ordinary people, it
    matches my inner thoughts
the moulding designer starts drafting economic policy and
    advancing the system of roads
finding the main points on an iron sheet, the center of
    iron, organizing principles,
the thread-cutter is busy with plans and development,
    planning a development zone on an iron sheet
the central zone, where they forge a subpar financial
    center, the sharp whistle of the machines
is the demolition of the last holdouts' houses and their
    relocation, the hardware factory's polisher,
hole-puncher, and cutter, who live with their relatives in
    one room, use a ruthless measure
to mould iron lives, they are confined there to polish,
    punch, and bore
the size and depth must be harmonious and stable, the
    textbooks repeat the political ideology

they must learn forbearance, this is a separate China of
    unemployment, layoffs,
job injuries, severed fingers, uncouth people prevented
    from living in the city
the representatives give speeches, the Central Consultative
    Conference puts forward proposals, while elementary
    students explain in their homework
that to create a clean and tourist-friendly city, migrant
    workers must be forbidden from crowding in
they live the shame of an iron-sheet nation, so many of
    their hearts are weak
they can't take x pounds of pain, they get stomach
    problems and occupational diseases
and kidney stones, their blood vessels are filled with
    dissatisfaction and grudges, made sick for this iron nation
bringing elements of destabilization, and petitioners begin
    to enter the next process
product inspectors begin to pick undesirables, familiar
    iron pieces show another face
the scarred competitors, it's overly humorous and righ-
    teous, not yielding
to a single doctrine, and we begin to use computer bits and
    forms to express happiness
time is like a meat-filled cake, it lacks a birthplace and an
    identity, it is stuffed with too much dissent
we must wait for the cleaners to come and clean, this iron
    will replace its tongue and mouth
it fits in well with a chorus, it uses satire and rhetorical
    tricks
to recite the comedies of life, while the bureaucratic
    outside quality control has only one direction
she starts to criticize the iron nation, her voice is filled
with spiritualism and alchemy, this iron needs better
    political ideology,

along with the poetry and art of existence, iron is too quiet
it hasn't cast off the old customs, it won't face the
    consumer gods
and flirt, it needs revisions and deletions and for time to
    return
to the 1990s, our transformations need to be examined
    anew
these restless years need to be debated and misunderstandings
must be corrected, iron's moulds are stuck in the 1980s
its dull stiff circles don't work in the new age, the moulding
    designers need
to be woken up, they've stood too long in the advantages
    of the past
or they're too close to the bureaucrats of old and the VIPs
    of the present
their designs aren't right for the masses, the thread-cutter
    cares too much
about profits, leaving out the curved lines of ordinary
    people, leaving the polishers,
hole-punchers, and cutters responsible for the inferior
    goods, and the suffering
indecisive, iron's despair puts the responsibility on dead
    politicians, and just as we
have never felt grief beyond reason, the dead offer pardon
to reach memories and symbols even emptier than iron's
    political party, the bosses
pay respects to useless objects, the statisticians calculate
    mistakes and defects
her handwriting distorts, it makes my pay seem complex
    and confusing
sickening my heart, and under the stare of collectivism we
    learn
how to distrust, habit and lack of habit replace force, I
    think rebellion

must play the role of a loyal worker, punching the time
    clock right on time, respectful of superiors
thoughts washed clean by iron's political party, there are
    eyes everywhere
it glistens in light like pliers, gripping excess thinking and
    imagination
the security guards are good at violence, guarding the doors
    and searching bodies, their blue uniforms
are as forbidding as policemen's, they inspect the work-
    shops, hand out fines to those they find napping

Now I return to the center of iron, and where does it come
    from—
a mountain's depths, a coal mine, from outside the country,
    it was once in buried stone
dug up, pulverized, it contains the earth's coughing
its dark grey body is wracked by late-stage disease, iron's past
is so desolate I don't dare imagine any more, it has passed
    through tall buildings, factories,
railways and state-run processing plants, it is installed
    even deeper in the machines than the earth
its hopes need the hacksaw and spark machine, I use a
    mute language to speak
of its desires, returning to the mind of rocks, it can't speak
    Chinese
the hardest place of the Han, I can only indistinctly hear
    its sound like rocks
crying, it comes from a hand-dug cellar, and the way back
    has been sealed up by industry and city management
it's traveling a corridor made of non-fiction, from stone to
    iron
from iron to product, it encounters nonstop time
it is cut into incomplete shapes, of yesterday, today,
    tomorrow,

history, the future, the present, or the twenty-first century,
    it's all fragments of you
or me, you want to hold onto the old doctrines, tossed
    around by life, pushed aside
life can't tolerate overly perfect things, it has a dangerous
jealous heart, the beginning is the end, and I'm still longing
    for ancient times as I stand at this modern machine
longing to go back to the Tang—to write poetry, collect
    Chinese medicine on the mountainsides, go fishing in
    the wind and fine rain

Index of Chinese Titles

Acknowledgments

Some of the poems in this collection first appeared in *Chinese Literature Today* (Vol. 10, issue 2), *Poetry and Conflict: An Anthology of the Hong Kong International Poetry Nights 2019* (Hong Kong: The Chinese University Press, 2019) and *Iron Moon: An Anthology of Chinese Migrant Worker Poetry* (Buffalo: White Pine Press, 2017).

ZUZANNA GINCZANKA FIREBIRD
Translated by Alissa Valles

PERE GIMFERRER *Translated by Adrian Nathan West*

W. S. GRAHAM *Selected by Michael Hofmann*

SAKUTARŌ HAGIWARA CAT TOWN
Translated by Hiroaki Sato

MICHAEL HELLER TELESCOPE: SELECTED POEMS

MIGUEL HERNÁNDEZ *Selected and translated by Don Share*

RICHARD HOWARD RH ♥ HJ AND OTHER AMERICAN WRITERS
Introduction by Timothy Donnelly

LI SHANGYIN *Edited and translated by Chloe Garcia Roberts*

AT THE LOUVRE POEMS BY 100 CONTEMPORARY WORLD POETS

ARVIND KRISHNA MEHROTRA *Selected by Vidyan Ravinthiran;
Introduction by Amit Chaudhuri*

HENRI MICHAUX A CERTAIN PLUME
Translated by Richard Sieburth; Preface by Lawrence Durrell

MELISSA MONROE MEDUSA BEACH

EUGENIO MONTALE LATE MONTALE
Selected and translated by George Bradley

HENRI MICHAUX A CERTAIN PLUME
Translated by Richard Sieburth; Preface by Lawrence Durrell

ÁLVARO MUTIS MAQROLL'S PRAYER AND OTHER POEMS
Translated by Chris Andrews, Edith Grossman, and Alastair Reid

VIVEK NARAYANAN AFTER

SILVINA OCAMPO *Selected and translated by Jason Weiss*